OUR
GOD
SPEAKS

MEET THE LOVING FATHER WHO
LONGS TO ANSWER YOUR PRAYERS

CLELAND
THOM

BY THE SAME AUTHOR

MOSES, THE MAKING OF A LEADER. Published by Kingsway in the UK and Victory Press in America. Book of the Day at Spring Harvest.

ABRAHAM, FRIEND OF GOD. Published by Kingsway.

BROKEN HEARTED BELIEVERS. Published by Kingsway in the UK and Karas Sana in Finland.

FRIENDS OF GOD. Co-written with Jeff Lucas. Published by Crossway.

THE POWER TO PERSUADE. Published by Pioneer.

DESTINY CALLS, first edition. Published by Canaan Press. Ghost-written for Norman and Grace Barnes.

QUESTIONABLE SUPERNATURAL. Published by Amazon.

DESTINY CALLS, second edition. Published by Clean Copy Editing. Ghost-written for Norman and Grace Barnes.

THE PATH OF THE SEER. Published by Amazon.

THE CHURCH THAT JESUS BUILT. Published by Amazon.

DONATIONS

I don't make any money from my books, podcasts, or resources.

Anything you paid for this book covers Amazon's fees. All other income goes to Ray of Sunshine House, a family home for previously vulnerable children near Cape Town, South Africa.

If you received a free copy, then please consider donating to them via PayPal:

https://www.paypal.com/paypalme/rayofsunshinehouse

DEDICATION

They're called the Banana Bunch. Why? For no reason at all!

They are faithful, gifted, experienced and love to laugh.

Over the past three years, they have met over 900 times, to selflessly pray for people they don't even know.

They sometimes convene at moment's notice as people battle with death and trauma. They have saved many lives with their prayers and have seen God perform at least 200 miracles.

They prove that the prayers of righteous men and women are powerful and effective (James 5: 16). They also demonstrate how to bear fruit in old age.

This book is their story. Meet the Banana Bunch:

- Steph Armstrong.
- Keith and Carole Berkley.
- Amy Blackburn.
- Gill Cranch.
- David and Sue Frankland.
- Karen Hutchins.
- Robyn Lofthouse.
- Jan Maloney.
- Reg and Ann Smith.
- Elaine Stewart.
- Jake Thom.
- Frank and Jeannette Thorpe.

CONTENTS

INTRODUCTION

There's a new religion invading a church near you.

It's called the Religion of Unanswered Prayer. You can even buy books and go on courses to learn about it.

Followers have a 'story' about why God didn't answer a prayer. It's all part of their 'journey.' Like it's something to celebrate.

And this faithless, powerless philosophy proclaims to a desperate world: 'Come and meet the God who doesn't speak.'

How depressing.

In contrast, the Bible reveals prayers that changed history. People were healed, enemies defeated, prison doors opened, and lions' mouths closed.

Nothing's changed. Father God still hears, still speaks, and still answers. He wants to resolve your impossibilities.

This book invites you to meet him.

It's not theory. It's backed up with more than 200 miracles, signs and wonders that God performed when a few people from Freedom Church started praying three years ago.

A revival? No. According to the Bible, it's God's normal.

A 'journey'? Yes, though more like a white-knuckle ride with the Jesus we had not met before.

Come and see.

Cleland Thom
August 2022

CHAPTER 1

GOD HAS NOT LOST HIS VOICE

Jesus didn't teach about unanswered prayer. What a relief.

Instead, he said: 'If you believe, you will receive whatever you ask for in prayer' (Matthew 21: 22).

And he added: 'Whatever you ask for in prayer, believe that you have received it, and it will be yours' (Mark 11: 24).

He also promised: 'Ask and it will be given to you; seek and you will find; knock and the door will be opened to you' (Matthew 7: 7).

And then, he told a parable about persevering in prayer (Luke 11: 5-8) and told us to use mustard seeds of faith to move mountains (Mark 11: 23).

So, God listens, and answers. Well, of course he does!

Why would anyone follow a silent God? That would make him a 'mute idol' (1 Corinthians 12: 2). The world has plenty of those already.

The God of the Bible spoke the universe into being in Genesis 1 and has spoken to imperfect and undeserving people like us ever since. He spoke to Adam and Eve before they sinned, and afterwards.

He called Jesus the word, not the Blank Space or the Silence.

And Jesus spoke to people like Judas, even as he handed him over to Roman soldiers to be arrested. He spoke to a guilty thief on a cross, and an immoral woman at a well. He spoke to his enemies, his friends, his followers, and his disciples.

He spoke to the religious and the reckless, to rabbis and ruffians, Pharisees, and prostitutes. He even spoke to Satan when he had to.

And then he was willingly crucified so you can speak to him boldly and confidently whenever you want to (Hebrews 4: 16).

He loves to reply.

WE NEED TO TALK

Jesus was also called Emmanuel (Matthew 1: 23), which means *God with us*. And he is *with us* to talk, not to sit in awkward silence like in a dentist's waiting room.

He still invites you to have breakfast with him when you fail (John 21). He still tells outcasts: 'I must stay at your house today' (Luke 19: 5) when others avoid them or cancel them.

Jesus also said: 'Anyone who has seen me has seen the Father' (John 14: 9). So, Father God is as keen to chat to people as Jesus is. He is the lover who pursues his bride and speaks beauty to her (Song of Songs 4).

He will speak to you in many ways, especially when you read your Bible. In fact, no one can say he is silent if they have a Bible.

This book comprises around 783,137 living, active, God-breathed words that carry life, healing, instruction, comfort, promises and answers to every human need. So, if God seems to have gone quiet, pick up your Bible and keep reading it until he says: 'Hello.'

In the parable of the sower (Matthew 13: 13), there were plenty of words. But people couldn't hear them because their hearts were hard. It's easy to become like that. You hear, but don't 'hear' and don't understand God's ways or recognise his voice. But that doesn't mean he's silent.

Or maybe you erect barriers through disobedience and blame God for your blocked ears or make a religion out of your deafness. But the truth is, God wants to share romantic intimacy with you.

MORE THAN JUST GOOD FRIENDS

Talking to God is called prayer. And the Hebrew word for prayer is *tefilah*. It means asking for things. The word also includes the meanings of *worshipping him, thanking him, praising him, communing with him and confessing things to him.*

It comes from the Hebrew root *palal*, which means to *think, to judge, to differentiate, to clarify, and decide.*

So, pray is an opportunity to confess things, judge situations, differentiate between right and wrong, and make decisions – all in conversation with the creator of the universe.

And as you become his friend, you can influence him, like Abraham did when he pleaded for the city of Sodom in Genesis 18: 23-32. Your prayers can change lives and situations. They can change history. That's when it gets exciting.

But first, you may need to face an uncomfortable truth.

PRAYER MEETINGS ... WHY BOTHER?

I've been involved with various prayer groups over the years.

One should have met at the Waffle House. One could have been called the Ramblers Association. Another had a contract with Talk Talk. One was populated with drones.

You get my point! Meetings like these waste people's time. And God's. He's probably as bored with them as you are.

But the time for waffling, rambling, talking, and droning is over. Our depraved and diseased world yearns to hear God speak about their sicknesses, their broken families, and give hope to their confused and frightened children.

If you can't find a prayer meeting that is filled with faith, power, and God's presence, then take Jesus' advice and start your own. He said: 'Where two or three gather in my name, there am I with them' (Matthew 18: 19-20).

He didn't say you must ask a leader's permission or go on a course. Just gather and he'll join you. And then wait to see what he says.

POWER PICKS

- The Bunch prayed for a woman who was facing a colostomy after being diagnosed with bowel cancer.

  But God healed her by the time surgeons operated. They were surprised to discover that the cancerous tumours had disappeared.

  And a biopsy later showed that all the tissue samples were free of cancer, too.

- A man had serious heart problems and couldn't get upstairs or do the gardening. But after the Bunch prayed, he climbed the stairs normally, and without losing his breath. He was so surprised, he did it again!

  Subsequent hospital blood tests were 'normal'. The consultant said his heart was running like a smooth car engine and that he was one of the fittest 82-year-olds he had met.

  The consultant also took him off tablets for diabetes. And the man started gardening again!

- The Bunch prayed for a man who suffered from psychotic attacks and was jailed for 18 months for arson. He then spent eight years in a secure unit.

  But the psychotic episodes stopped after the Bunch prayed for him, and he is now well enough to live in a halfway house and serve in his local church.

CHAPTER 2

HOW DO YOU PRAY?

Prayer is easy. All you need is a room with a door.

Jesus said in Matthew 6: 6: 'Go into a room, shut the door and pray.' That's it.

He even gave you a sample prayer: 'Our Father in heaven, hallowed be your name, your kingdom come, your will be done, on earth as it is in heaven.

'Give us today our daily bread. And forgive us our debts, as we also have forgiven our debtors. And lead us not into temptation but deliver us from the evil one.'

Even I can pray that in an empty room with the door shut. It takes about 30 seconds.

God does not like long prayers. Jesus said in Matthew 6: 7: 'When you pray, do not keep on babbling like pagans.

They think they will be heard because of their many words.'

There should be a large notice on every church wall: '**Do not babble like pagans!'**

Jesus prayed the longest prayer in the Bible in John 17. It was only around 630 words. I'm only getting into my stride by then!

The rest are all under 200 words. Most are fewer than 100 words. The Lord's prayer is just 62 words. God prefers brevity. After all, he created the universe in around 120 words.

NOW LISTEN CAREFULLY

After you have shut the door and spent 30 seconds praying, wait for God to answer. He will. He promises in Jeremiah 33: 3: 'Call me and I will answer.'

And this is all you need to know about prayer. No audio, conference or teacher can explain it better than Jesus did. In fact, if you stop reading this book now, you know enough.

And if you have not got a room with a door, then find somewhere where you can shut everyone and everything out.

It can be tough to begin with. When I first tried it, I nearly went mad after a few minutes away from my iPhone. But then, Father started to speak. He'll do the same with you.

But what if he doesn't? Jesus covered that in Matthew 6, too.

1. JESUS SAID, WHEN YOU PRAY, NOT IF

Jesus spoke to all kinds of people. But he only shared secrets with his **disciples** (Mark 10: 32). So, he may not say much if you're just a casual acquaintance.

A ComRes Survey conducted by Tearfund in 2019, found that 27% of Christians had never prayed. But Martin Luther said: 'To be a Christian without prayer is no more possible than to be alive without breathing.'

So, you may need to change your prayer life from **if** to **when** if God seems silent.

2. PRAY EVERY DAY

Jesus' prayer sample says: 'Give us **today** our daily bread.' God doesn't do weekly orders so you can pop some spare loaves in the freezer.

When God's people were in the wilderness, he rained bread down on them every morning (Exodus 16). But it was only enough for that day. It became infested with maggots if they stored it overnight.

God's bread still goes mouldy. Daily bread is still the staple diet for God's people.

But what is God's bread? First, it's his word. Jesus said in Matthew 4: 4: 'Man shall not live on bread alone, but on every **word** that comes from the mouth of God.'

It also represents our healing and deliverance (Mark 7: 27).

And bread is Jesus' body (John 5: 53, 1 Corinthians 11: 24) and it will spiritually nourish you when you eat it in faith. How? I don't know. It just does. That's where faith comes in.

So, try to pray every day, or else you will miss God's delivery.

3. YOU GO FIRST ...

Jesus also said in Matthew 6: 'Shut the door and pray.' He prefers you to start the conversation. And when you do, he will draw near (James 4: 6).

It really is that easy.

At first, the conversation may be superficial, like chatting to a new person in church. But it changes when you know them better.

Psalm 42: 7 says: 'Deep calls unto deep'. So, if you go deep with God, he will go deep with you. But he won't force you. It takes time to build a deeper relationship with Father. But it's worth it.

4. MAKE SURE YOU'RE A SHEEP

Jesus said in John 10: 4 that his sheep know his voice. So, if you haven't experienced that, you may need to ask God: 'Am I a sheep?' If you have strayed from the sheep pen and gone your own way, then you won't be able hear him.

Or maybe you entered the pen 'some other way' like Jesus said to the Pharisees (John 10: 1).

Sheep pens in those days had high walls and one gate. The shepherd decided who came in, and intruders had to climb over the wall. Climbing involves effort. That's called religion.

Religious people try to get into the pen through ceremonies, rituals, or self-improvement rather than by faith. And so, they can't recognise the shepherd's voice. But that's not God's fault.

Perhaps it's time to tell him that you're serious – you want to be his sheep. Then start listening to his voice.

5. EXPECT A REWARD

Jesus promised in Matthew 6: 6 that his Father rewards people who pray. And Hebrews 11: 6 confirms it. It says God rewards those who earnestly seek him.

This reward may be an answer to a prayer, or something else. Father God decides. But any reward from God is worth having. Don't miss out!

6. WHO'S IN CHARGE?

When Jesus taught his disciples the Lord's prayer, he included the words: 'Your will be done.' Later, he prayed those words himself in the Garden of Gethsemane and it cost him his life.

Lordship is fundamental to hearing God speak. You can 'claim' answers all you like, but he is Lord and will answer when and how he wants.

Jesus' dearest friend John explained it in 1 John 5: 14: 'This is the confidence which we have before Him, that, if we ask anything according to his will, he hears us.'

SUBMIT YOUR CLAIM?

Some teaching makes **you** Lord. It says you can claim whatever you want. But this fundamentally misunderstands God. You can't claim anything. He is Lord, and you must surrender to his will in each situation.

You don't find anyone 'claiming' anything in the Bible, apart from people in the first church in Jerusalem. Acts 4: 32 says: 'No one **claimed** that any of their possessions was their own, but they shared everything they had.'

A very different emphasis!

Some faith teaching is founded on paranormal techniques discovered by a non-Christian called Phineas Quimby, an 18th century mental healer and hypnotist. He believed that faith was a mind-over-matter **force** that could be activated by words.

A woman named Mary Baker Eddy followed his teaching and founded the cult of Christian science. And the word of Faith Movement introduced it into the Christianity.

It works. But that doesn't make it right. And it's not a 'counterfeit', because no one followed this practice in the Bible.

I've met Christians who have claimed things like a luxury home or money for an expensive holiday, and then confessed a Bible verse until they got it. But those answers may not have come from God.

How can you tell? James 4: 3 says: 'You ask and do not receive, because you ask with wrong motives, so that you may spend it on your pleasures.'

The Greek word for *pleasures* means *sensual pleasures.* So, if you claim anything for physical enjoyment, the answer doesn't come from God, as he won't contradict his word.

So, you should then ask: 'Where **did** it come from?' Let me tell you. Try searching the internet for 'Positive confessions to attract wealth' and you will find large numbers of websites that teach you how to get rich by declaring money confessions.

But they are not Christian. Quite the opposite. They are nothing to do with God and the Bible.

Prayer isn't a method and faith isn't a formula. It's a walk with a friend – Father God, who has the right to say no, or wait, or who won't respond until you put something right.

I knew a woman who 'claimed' that she would live a long life. But I told her: 'It probably won't happen.' She was shocked, but I explained that God only promised her a long life if she honoured her parents (Exodus 20: 12). She frequently criticised hers. So, the chances were that she would die young unless she repented.

No amount of confession will change God's laws.

I AM NOT IM

God doesn't always provide rapid replies like Instant Messaging. He's Jehovah, not Alexa.

Satan offered Adam and Eve instant answers in the Garden of Eden (Genesis 3: 5). 'Your eyes will be opened, and you will be like God, knowing good and evil,' he said. No waiting, no seeking. And look how it ended.

It took God around 430 years to respond to the Jewish people's pleas for a release from slavery (Exodus 12: 40-41). Why? His timing is perfect. Anything quicker is a bonus!

God sometimes makes you wait, to assess your heart, or because you are not ready to hear what he says. Or he answers by saying No. He can do that because he is Lord.

Jesus isn't a mute Messiah or a silent saviour. And God isn't the Lord with laryngitis.

He listens, and answers by speaking to us personally like he always has done. And it starts when you go into a room and shut the door.

POWER PICKS

- One man sliced part of his thumb off at work. The Bunch prayed it would grow back, and when he went to have the remainder amputated, the doctors were astonished that it was growing again. They cancelled the amputation.

- The Bunch prayed for an elderly lady who had been bedridden for over two years with grave heart and kidney problems. She also suffered from severe lymphedema, which caused bad swellings all over her body. She needed her legs dressed twice a day.

  First, the doctors were puzzled when her heart rate normalised. Then her kidney function improved, and the swellings started going down.

  Within months, she lost nine stone – half her body weight – and began going out and living a normal life again.

- God healed a man who was expected to die from pancreatic cancer. Doctors told his wife and children that he was unlikely to survive for long.

  But the Bunch prayed, and scans showed that the cancerous growth had disappeared. The man was only diagnosed with jaundice, and Father healed that straight away when the Bunch prayed again.

  Within a few weeks, he felt so well he started decorating his house.

- She suffered from aspiration pneumonia and hadn't been out of hospital for more than 17 consecutive days since around 2005.

I prayed with her over the phone. We broke some curses, and God healed her. Her lungs cleared completely. She has not been readmitted to hospital for breathing problems since then.

The Holy Spirit also healed her asthma.

However, she was still in chronic pain from prolapsed and herniated discs, osteoarthritis, osteoporosis, trapped nerves in her spine from the neck down, and worsening stenosis. She could only walk a few paces with the aid of a walking frame and used opioids to combat the pain.

God show me a satanic strong man influencing her life, so I bound it according to Mark 3:27. She did not know I had prayed but dreamt that night she could walk. The following day, she woke up free of pain and discovered she had been healed. She walked unaided around a farm and climbed a flight of stairs at her church.

She gradually stopped her medication – 38 tablets a day – and travelled on a train for the first time in 18 years. God also healed her of mental illness, and she was discharged after 53 years' treatment.

Later, she was healed of a hernia that she had suffered with for 28 years and regained her sight. She had been blind since was she a little girl.

She continues to live a full and active life. All her healings have been verified by doctors.

CHAPTER 3

GOD WANTS A WORD

Let's settle something. The Bible is God's preferred method of communication. So, if you think he's gone quiet, maybe you should read it more often.

His son, Jesus **is** the word and without it, your faith will collapse.

In Luke 6: 46-49 Jesus described two types of builders. A wise one built his spiritual house on rock. But a foolish one build it on sand, and it collapsed when life's storms struck.

Jesus then explained that the wise builder had heard God's word and put it into practice.

Of course, God speaks in other ways – through dreams and visions, prophecies, quietly in your heart, through other people, through signs, or through apparent coincidences. But these are not rocks. They are not the Jesus, the word.

THE FINAL WORD

Father God has said everything that he needs to say in scripture. You won't find anything new anywhere else.

That's why Paul told his apprentice Timothy that the Bible is **God-breathed** (2 Timothy 3: 16-17), a dynamic term that is only used to describe God's word.

Paul adds that it is useful for ... 'teaching, rebuking, correcting, and training in righteousness, so that we may be thoroughly equipped for every good work'.

Only God's word can equip you thoroughly for Christian work. That's why many people fall away under pressure. Perhaps they were built on prophecies, choruses, signs, courses, and conferences. These are good. But they are not the word.

So, let's find out more about this incredible book.

1. THE BIBLE IS EASY TO UNDERSTAND

If you think the Bible is difficult, dull, or boring then you need to get your heart right. Yes, really.

In the parable of sower (Matthew 13: 1-23) Jesus uses seeds to represent God's word, and soil to represent your heart. And he explained that God's word won't produce fruit if your heart is hard.

Then he recalled Isaiah 6: 9-10, which said people's hearts were hard because they had ignored God's word. And he concluded: 'He who has ears to hear, let him hear.'

This applies to us. God's word will only take root if you have obeyed it in the past. It's your responsibility. It's up to you whether you have 'ears to hear'.

2. THE BIBLE IS FOR THE UNEDUCATED

I used to help to lead a church in the poorest area of London. Many people in the congregation were uneducated and some could scarcely read. But many of them understood the Bible because their hearts were right.

Some of their insights astounded scholars. But that isn't surprising, as God says in Psalm 19:7 that his word is for the **simple.**

The Hebrew word for simple means *someone who lacks intellectual ability and sound judgment and who is prone to making mistakes and being led astray.*

So, who is simple? Me, for starters. And maybe you.

Crowds of 'common people' listened to Jesus with delight when he preached in Matthew 12: 3. They were simple. Some of Jesus' disciples were simple, too. Peter and John were described as 'uneducated, common men' in Acts 4: 13.

But Jesus still expected them to understand God's word and asked them things like: 'Have you not read in the scripture …?'

In contrast, educated Jewish scholars and teachers couldn't grasp his teaching because their hearts were hard.

3. THE BIBLE IS A POWER TOOL

I bought a new iPhone last year and didn't read the instruction manual. So, I only recently discovered that it did more than I realised. Similarly, you won't discover what God can do unless you read his instruction manual.

The Bible has unique power, but only if you use it with faith. Many Christians don't bother and then wonder why they have a monochrome prayer life.

4. THE BIBLE IS 100% RELIABLE

Psalm 119: 89 says that God's word stands firm in the heavens. That's reassuring when everything on our planet – including the planet itself – is increasingly shaky.

It stands firm because it's God's word, not ours. It's untainted by anything, or anyone. It's perfect. And it doesn't have a use-by date. So, the content in the Bible on your shelf or on your device will outlast heaven and earth (Matthew 21: 23).

Keep this in mind when you hear dire warnings about climate change. The doom mongers are right – the earth will be destroyed. But God promises in his word to create a new one (Isaiah 65: 17 and Revelation 21: 1). And he will. I don't hear many climate change clerics mentioning this at the moment.

5. THE BIBLE DOESN'T CHANGE

We live in a society where most people 'do their own thing'. It's nothing new. Judges 21:25 says: 'All the people did whatever seemed right in their own eyes.'

In contrast, God invites us to do **his** thing. And any society that goes its own way will be blighted by war, drought, poverty, sickness, injustice, crime, and hatred. Just look around.

God's word never changes, and never will. It was finished and settled before creation. So, you don't have to decide if something is right or wrong. God has already settled it. You just have to decide if you agree. It's up to you. Father allows you to decide, and to 'take offence' if you want to.

However, God's word isn't settled on earth. Throughout history, people have distorted it, changed it, mistranslated it, and tried to destroy it. They still do.

Some adapt it according to prevailing doctrines like political correctness, and then persecute those who disagree. It's already happening in the UK and will get worse.

But history proves that the persecutors and compromisers are wasting their time. God's word stands for ever.

6. THE BIBLE CAN SORT YOU OUT

The Bible's the best place to go for a spiritual health check.

Hebrews 4:12 says: 'The word of God is alive and active. Sharper than any double-edged sword, it penetrates even to dividing soul and spirit, joints, and marrow; it judges the thoughts and attitudes of the heart.'

How does that work? Well, read Romans 12: 8-19, Galatians 5: 19-21 and the ten commandments (Exodus 20: 1-17). Then list the areas where you fall short. You won't find a better plumbline.

7. THE BIBLE IS EFFECTIVE

Psalm 119 says in various places that God's word provides counsel, victory, comfort, revival, physical and emotional healing, protection, and salvation.

And elsewhere the Bible promises spiritual life, spiritual growth, prosperity, healing, and guidance, and is a spiritual weapon. You will see unimaginable miracles and answers to prayer when you use the word and Spirit together.

Sadly, many prominent church leaders in the 1980s and 1990s publicly questioned the authority of God's word. They were fools. And if that wasn't enough, the wonderful Toronto revival led to a deceptive focus on the Holy Spirit and his so-called manifestations.

And so, Jesus the word has been pushed aside for around 30 years and our churches have become weak, secularised, and ineffective.

But you can start to put that right today, by learning to love God's word. It will change your prayer life. In fact, it will change your whole life, and other people's.

8. THE BIBLE IS UNIQUE

God's word isn't limited by time or space. Psalm 119: 96 says: 'Your commandment is boundless.' And here's some proof.

Humankind first discovered that the earth was round in 500 BC.

But the Bible had already established this two centuries earlier. Isaiah (42: 20) wrote that God 'sits enthroned above the **circle** of the earth'. And Job 26: 10 says: 'He has inscribed a **circle** on the surface of the waters at the boundary of light and darkness.'

Similarly, a scientist named Galileo Galilei proved that air had weight in 1600 AD. But the Bible revealed that God 'imparted weight to the wind' centuries earlier, in 600 BC (Job 28:25).

You can find further proof from the books that were written by Old Testament prophets.

The authors probably didn't know each other or read each others' work. They lived in different locations, and their writings spanned around 320 years.

Yet many prophesied a Messiah, without contradiction. Some of their writings were the same, almost word for word. And around 300 of their prophecies about Jesus have come true. Humanly, this is all impossible.

The Bible is an immense book of truth and love. That's why everyone from governments to wokes hate it. If it had no power, they'd ignore it.

So, how can you hear God speak through his word? We all study differently, but these fundamentals can apply to most of us.

1. READ IT WITH JESUS

The Bible isn't a bullet-point list of instructions. Jesus will speak to you as you walk with him. He **unfolded** the scriptures to two discouraged disciples on the road to Emmaus (Luke 24: 27), so they understood what was going on.

He will do the same with you when you least expect it.

2. READ IT WITH THE HOLY SPIRIT

You won't benefit from the Bible without the Holy Spirit's help. Paul said in 1 Corinthians 2: 6-14: 'The Spirit searches all things, even the deep things of God.

'What we have received isn't the spirit of the world, but the Spirit who is from God, so that we may understand what God has freely given us.

'This is what we speak, not in words taught us by human wisdom but in words taught by the Spirit, explaining spiritual realities with Spirit-taught words.

'The person without the Spirit does not accept the things that come from the Spirit of God but considers them foolishness and can't understand them because they are discerned only through the Spirit.'

This doesn't mean that you set aside your intellect. But you need the Holy Spirit to teach you. Jesus told his disciples in John 16: 3: 'But when He, the Spirit of truth comes, he will guide you into all truth; for he will not speak on his own initiative.'

So, before you read the Bible, ask the Holy Spirit to teach you, to show you what he wants to do in your life, and how he wants you to change.

3. PLAY HIDE AND SEEK

God hid his face from people like Job (Job 13: 24), Ethan the Ezrahite (Psalm 89: 46), and King David (Psalm 30: 7).

Why? To make them hungry and learn perseverance. He will sometimes do the same with you. It's like a divine game of hide and seek.

So, if he is silent, tell him: 'Ready or not, here I come!' and start searching for him. You will find him, because Jeremiah 29: 23 says: 'If you look for me wholeheartedly, you will find me.' He is worth finding!

4. LEARN TO BE PATIENT

Listening top God can take time. He gives revelation from the tree of life, not information from the tree of knowledge. He speaks out of relationship, not like a divine Alexa, who just passes on second hand information.

Romans 10: 17 says: 'Faith comes by hearing God's word.' The Greek word *comes* means to *emerge from the inside*, like giving birth. In contrast, books, manuals, and websites are external sources and are not where faith **comes** from.

Don't settle for second best.

Psalm 130 starts with the writer – probably King David – crying out to the Lord from the depths. Not a great place to be. And he didn't get an instant message – v6-7 reveal that he had to wait and learn how to live in the waiting room.

Jesus had perfect communion with his Father, but still spent all night praying about which disciples to choose (Luke 6: 12-13). The names didn't just appear instantly in his inbox.

So, if God appears to be slow to speak, don't worry. He's answering but taking his time.

WORD PERFECT

You can't know or love Jesus without knowing and loving the Bible. They're one and the same. John 1: 14 says: 'The word became flesh and made his dwelling among us.' He was referring to Jesus. The perfect word.

And if you learn to love him by using his word, you will discover: 'It is he who reveals the profound and hidden things; he knows what is in the darkness, and the light dwells with him' (Daniel 2: 22).

POWER PICKS

- A church pastor was seriously in in hospital with COVID. The Bunch prayed, and he recovered so quickly that he was able to start prayer meetings in his hospital ward before being sent home. He shared God's word and prayed for doctors, nurses, and patients.

- A woman was immobile because of a severe back injury. We recorded prayers for her to pray, and later that day, God gave her a vision. She was immediately healed and got up and moved around freely. She even came to our church meeting the following day.

- The Bunch prayed for a lady who was in intensive care after a serious heart attack.

  Her internal organs were failing, and she wasn't expected to survive the night. But the Bunch prayed, God intervened, and she recovered.

  Later, tests showed she had no history of heart trouble, her kidney function had risen from a Growth Differentiation Factor level of zero (complete failure) to 50 and she was able to climb a flight of stairs. Seven days earlier, she couldn't manage to walk from her bed to a chair.

  God also healed her long-term anaemia, and her internal bleeding stopped. Doctors cancelled six weeks rehab because she didn't need it.

CHAPTER 4

DOING THINGS GOD'S WAY

Prayer is a personal conversation with your heavenly Father. But like any relationship, his answers will reflect what he's like. He isn't a machine.

He knows what you're like, but you must get to know him too. If you don't, you may misunderstand his answers to your prayers, and he may seem absent or unloving when you will face difficult situations.

The Bible refers to God's character as 'his ways'. And the Hebrew word *ways* has several meanings:

- It's a **road:** in this case, God's road.
- It's a **journey**: you go somewhere.
- And it's someone's **character**: the way they are.

So, to me, knowing God's ways means:

**Travelling with God on his road and
discovering what he's like as you go.**

During your journey, God will show you his values, what makes him pleased and what makes him angry. You will discover his impulses and understand his behaviour in different situations.

He may give you glimpses of his glory, tell you his opinion on the day's news or share some secrets with you. And as you walk with him, he will test you, because he wants you to reach your immense potential. And he may start to show you what he's doing in your life and why.

He'll let you see how he has worked in the past, so that your personal history makes sense. And when he does, you will understand why Isaiah 55: 8-9 says: 'For my thoughts are not your thoughts, neither are your ways my ways.'

God is utterly different from us.

His ways are drenched in his goodness, love, and mercy. But he can also seem to be offensive, outrageous, unreasonable, reckless, unfair, and illogical. He wouldn't – and doesn't – last long on university campuses. He will offend wokes, non-wokes and everyone in between.

CHARACTER STUDY

So, let's examine some aspects of God's unfathomable character. Prepare to be shocked. He may bear little resemblance to the God you have met before.

- He created the Garden of Eden with a protective hedge around it, but then allowed Satan the Snake to roam freely, knowing he had the capacity to kill, lie and steal.

  Would you put a snake in the garden while your kids were out playing?

- He said in Deuteronomy 23: 17-18: 'None of the daughters of Israel shall be a cult prostitute.' But then he placed Rahab the prostitute in Jesus' lineage (Matthew 1: 5), and later included her faith's Hall of Fame in Hebrews 11.

- He forbade incest in Leviticus 18: 7-18, but then placed Ruth in Jesus' lineage (Matthew 1: 5) too. She was a descendant of incest between Lot and his daughter.

- He also included lady named Bathsheba in Jesus' lineage. She was the 'other woman' (2 Samuel 11:4) in King David's marriage.

These examples show that God loves to work with repentant people who have faith. He loves to demonstrate how he can restore victims and bring purpose from pain to people like me, and you. His 'qualifications' bear no resemblance to ours.

Are you ready for some more?

- He gave firstborn sons special rights in Exodus 13: 12, but then discarded them with Jacob and Joseph. This seemed unfair and had devastating effects on Esau, and on Joseph's brothers.

- He sent an angel to free Peter from prison but didn't save James (Acts 12: 17) in identical circumstances. James was executed.

- Jesus revealed he was the Messiah to a woman who was an adulterer, a hated Samaritan, a reject, and an outcast.

  And then, he radically told her that believers could worship God anywhere, provided they did it in spirit and in truth. No more sacrifices or trips to the temple.

  Why tell her? He should have told Nicodemus, Israel's teacher. Instead, he told Nicodemus needed to be born again.

- God sent the tribe of Judah into battle in Judges 20, and 22,000 of them died. Then, he sent the remainder out a second time, and another 18,000 were killed. What kind of victory was that?

- He told his disciples to row a boat straight into a life-threatening storm, and then left them struggling desperately for several hours.

  He eventually walked towards them on the water ... to rescue them? Nope.

  The Greek text in Mark 6: 48 says that Jesus had **already resolved** to walk straight past them. He only changed his mind when the disciples cried out to him.

- He gave Jonah, a **disobedient** prophet, a successful ministry. But John the Baptist, an **obedient** prophet, was jailed and beheaded.

- He told his people that divination was detestable in Deuteronomy 18: 10, but then allowed three astrologers to visit baby Jesus. Their visit resulted in the slaughter of hundreds of babies.

And if that's not enough:

- He sent his son to earth in human form by causing a young teenage girl to fall pregnant when she was already engaged.

- He introduced his son to the world as an illegitimate, surrogate, homeless refugee, and was fathered by a man who wasn't his biological dad.

- He is a Holy God who can't look at sin but sent Jesus to befriend drunks, thieves, prostitutes, and outcasts. Today he would probably meet with terrorists, paedophiles, people who have been cancelled ... and those who cancelled them.

GOD ISN'T YOU

So, God's ways may seem irresponsible and unfair. Why? Because he isn't us. He is I AM. He doesn't have to explain or justify himself to anyone. And he is wiser and sees a bigger picture than you ever could.

Sometimes, he behaves irrationally because he is madly in love with you. That's what lovers do. But he'll also deeply offend you to expose your wrong attitudes, and he'll treat you unfairly to encourage you to mature.

He's shocking. He is unpredictable. He will even wash your feet and send his son to die for you. And if you've asked him to be your Lord, you can't stop him, because he can't break his repeated promise not to leave you or forsake you (Joshua 1: 5, Deuteronomy 31: 6, Hebrews 13: 5).

So, your prayer life will only make sense when you understand God's ways.

He isn't interested in inhabiting your culture or adapting to your ways. He may be unlike the sanitised and sensible God you have met in church. He would be – and is – banned from most churches, either because he's too risky, or because he won't stick to their rules.

His ways are not canals that follow safe, risk-assessed routes. They are rivers that change course, get choppy, meander, and evolve according to circumstances.

The Israelites only saw his deeds because they had hard, selfish hearts. In contrast, Moses wanted to know God so much that he said in Exodus 33: 15: 'I'm not going anywhere without you.'

So, ask God to show you his ways. He will. But be prepared – the revelation will change everything. Especially your prayer life.

God's ways in your family

Praying for families can be tough. But as you understand God's ways, you will see him change impossible situations.

It starts by facing a tough fact: God chose your family.

Some people find this hard to accept. And I'm not minimising it. But that's the deal.

I was born into a family of spiritists and had an uncle who abused me. I wish it had been different, but Psalm 18: 30 says his ways are perfect. Who am I to disagree? And even if I do, what's the point? It doesn't change anything.

Jeremiah 1: 5 reveals that God knew Jeremiah **before** he formed him in the womb. So, he knew whose womb he was going to use. The same applies to you. But that isn't the end of the story. It's the start of another one.

Ephesians 1: 4 says he chose you before the creation of the world. And verse 5 explains: 'In love he predestined us for adoption to sonship through Jesus Christ.' That's the reason you're here – God wants to adopt you as his child. How good is that?

If you struggle to accept your parents or your family, ask God to reveal his ways. He will.

Your family probably isn't like the Waltons. But neither were most families in the Bible. In fact, it's hard to find a decent one. Adam and Eve's eldest boy, Cain set the standard. He killed his brother, Abel because he was jealous of him. And the pattern continued throughout the Old Testament, with violence, vendettas and villainy, rape, lies, plots, and deceit. Sound familiar? You're not alone.

Would you want Lot and his incestuous daughters in your house group? Or fancy hanging out with Joseph's barbaric brothers, or Eli's sex-mad sons?

We all have difficult family stuff. And privilege doesn't make us immune – ask Princes William and Harry. But learning God's ways mean he will put things right if you ask him to and he will show you unimaginable things too.

How? He starts with a covenant promise. In Genesis 12: 3 God told Abraham: 'All the families on earth will be blessed through you.' So, God has signed a legally binding contract to bless your family. And he will. Here's how it works.

JOSEPH'S TECHNICOLOUR EXAMPLE

Joseph's family was a mess. His father, Jacob made a mistake. He had a favourite and didn't hide it – Genesis 37: 3 says: 'He loved Joseph more than all his children.'

No wonder his brothers hated him. And like most favourites, Joseph was cocky and arrogant, and even grassed up his brothers when he was 17.

And so, they threw him in a pit, told their father he was dead, and sold him into slavery. The Waltons? No. God's people.

So, God's promise of a family blessing seemed in ruins. And it got worse. In Genesis 37 some traders took Joseph to Egypt and sold him as a slave to King Potiphar. Then he was falsely accused of indecent assault and put in prison.

But ten long years later God, acted. He elevated Joseph from a prison to a palace and then to be prime minister. His promise was taking shape.

Back in Canaan, God used a famine to catch Jacob's attention. Jacob sent Joseph's brothers to Egypt to get food and guess who was handing it out? Joseph. A tearful reunion followed.

All this didn't happen because Jacob and Rebekah brought their children up like the Waltons or attended a family seminar at Spring Harvest. It happened because God kept his covenant promise, despite a murder plot, separation, slavery, lies, seduction, and prison.

It took time, and the people involved suffered grief, injustice, prison, pain, and famine. But extreme situations sometimes need extreme measures.

God can do the same for you. His ways are perfect. Your famine may turn out to be a blessing. So, ask him to show you his ways in your family. And pray according to his covenant. It's unconditional and he can't break it. He will speak.

POWER PICKS

- A couple were estranged from their daughter and hadn't heard from her for 12 years. The Bunch prayed and waged spiritual warfare for 18 months and she finally contacted them, right out the blue. They met up a few months later, and now have a better relationship than they ever had.

- One woman suffered a bad cough for several months, but it went the day after the Bunch prayed.

- A woman had a breakthrough with weight loss and lost two stone in five weeks after the Bunch prayed for her.

- The Bunch prayed for a new-born baby boy who was seriously ill in an intensive care unit after his mother suffered preeclampsia. He improved, but doctors couldn't send him home until he could breathe without support. We prayed again and he was discharged the following morning.

CHAPTER 5

TYPES OF PRAYER

We use different types of conversations, depending on the circumstances.

If you meet a friend to catch-up about church, that's one type.

But if you need advice on a personal problem, the conversation will be deeper and more focused.

And if you call a friend saying: 'Help! My car's broken down,' it's a cry for help.

It's the same with God. He has a type of prayers for every occasion.

Paul mentions four of them in 1 Timothy 2: 2: 'I urge, then, first of all, that petitions, prayers, intercession and thanksgiving be made for all people.'

This book covers prayers. But let's look at the other three.

1. PETITIONS

A petition means asking someone in authority to do something. I once signed one, asking a bus company to move a local bus stop.

Petitioning God is the same: you ask him for something specific.

The word *petition* in Greek means a *heartfelt, personal, urgent need*. And you usually only ask for one thing. Jesus gave four examples in the Lord's prayer (Matthew 6: 9-13).

- Give us this day our daily bread.
- Forgive us our trespasses.
- Lead us not into temptation.
- Deliver us from the evil one.

Just a few words each. That's all you need.

In the Old Testament, a little-known man called Jabez used petitions, too. 1 Chronicles 4: 10 says: 'Jabez cried out to the God of Israel.' The Hebrew word for *cry out* means to *petition* or *to summon*. And he submitted four of them:

- Bless me.
- Enlarge my territory.

- Put your hand upon me.
- Keep me from evil.

And the passage adds: 'So, God granted what he requested.' All sorted in 14 words. And he didn't 'claim' anything.

I've prayed Jabez's petition most days for more than 25 years, and it has brought incredible results for me, my family, my business, and the church I help to lead.

It's not a formula. But when you pray it with faith, God will answer you like he did Jabez.

BABY TALK

There's another petition in Luke 1. An elderly couple named Zechariah and Elizabeth were childless and wanted a baby. So, they prayed.

One day, Zechariah was on duty in the temple when an angel appeared, and said: 'Do not be afraid, Zechariah; your prayer has been heard. Your wife Elizabeth will bear you a son.'

The Greek word for *prayer* here is *petition*. So, Zechariah had presented God with a heartfelt, personal, and urgent need, and God responded.

Zechariah and Elizabeth may have wondered why Father took so long to answer. But God saw the bigger picture.

Baby John's birth had to synchronise with Jesus' birth, with prophecy, with genealogy, and with history. Try to remember that when God is slow to answer your prayers. His delays are for a reason.

I submitted my first petition when my doctor told me that my serious back injury would either paralyse me or kill me. I wasn't a Christian, but I just said: 'God if you're real, heal me.' And he did. I woke up without any pain and invited Jesus into my life the same day.

WE, THE UNDERSIGNED ...

There's an example of a group petition in Acts 4: 29. The religious authorities arrested Peter and John for healing a disabled man. They released them, warning them not to speak about Jesus. Some chance!

Peter and John went back to their friends, and petitioned God. In Acts 4: 29 they said: 'Enable your servants to speak your word with great **boldness**.'

And God answered immediately. It says in verse 31: 'After they prayed, the place where they were meeting was shaken. And they were all filled with the Holy Spirit and spoke the word of God **boldly**.'

They petitioned for boldness and got it.

I once presented an urgent petition for a couple whose marriage was about to collapse. In desperation, I cried out: 'Lord, please do something.' God told me to present a petition. So, I asked him to heal their marriage.

Almost immediately, I saw a vision of Father signing a scroll, renewing their marriage covenant. The situation changed immediately. Their love flowed again, and I left them in each other's arms. Their marriage turned a corner that day.

Petitions are also a useful way of stopping `people 'babbling like Christians' in church prayer meetings. We would see many more answers and cover more subjects!

2. INTERCESSION – MIND THE GAP

I had no experience of intercession until around three years ago. Since then, I've interceded for several people. I'm a novice, but the results have been dramatic and unexpected.

When you intercede for someone, you don't pray for them or about them. You pray the things that they can't or won't pray themselves. This means getting involved in their stuff, the same as Jesus got involved in ours when he became a man.

The Old Testament gives powerful examples of intercession. Daniel cried out to God over Israel's sins. And he got involved – he included himself in the prayers. He didn't say, 'Hey Lord, I'm an intercessor, so me and you, we can fix this.' Instead, he confessed: 'I'm a sinner.'

He added in Daniel 9: 5: 'We have sinned. We have acted wickedly. We have not listened, we have rebelled … the shame belongs to us.'

Intercession means being **in** the thick of it.

Nehemiah prayed the same way. In Nehemiah 1: 6 he cried out: 'I confess the sins we Israelites, including myself and my father's family, have committed against you. We have acted very wickedly toward you. We have not obeyed the commands, decrees, and laws.'

So, you intercede as a sinner, who 'stands in the gap' for others. But not many people are willing to do it.

In Ezekiel 22: 30 the Lord said: 'I looked for someone among them who would build up the wall and stand before me in the gap on behalf of the land so I would not have to destroy it, but I found no one.'

He is still looking.

God was referring to a gap in a city's defensive walls that would allow an enemy to invade it, and either kill people, imprison them, or send them into exile.

DODGING BULLETS

So, intercessors stand in that gap – an exposed and vulnerable place. They stand in between the person and the enemy, or the person and God's anger.

It can be dangerous and costly. No wonder God couldn't find one in a whole nation. I believe he's looking for one in the United Kingdom right now. Many of us pray, but does anyone intercede?

Moses stood in the gap for his fellow Israelites. Psalm 106: 19ff describes how the Jewish people worshipped a home-made golden calf.

Verse 23 says: 'So, God said he would destroy them.' But it adds: 'Moses, his chosen one, stood in the gap before him to keep his wrath from destroying them.'

What did Moses pray? Exodus 32: 33 reveals: 'Please forgive their sin. But if not, then blot **me** out of the book you have written.' He was willing to take their punishment. That's true intercession. Are you prepared to lose your salvation to spare our nation from more suffering?

Paul was. In Romans 9: 2 he said: 'I wish that I myself were cursed and cut off from Christ for the sake of my people.'

Jesus was, too. Isaiah 53:12 says: 'He poured out his life unto death and was numbered with the transgressors.' When Jesus was crucified, he said: 'Me too. I'm a transgressor.' And he didn't stop there. Verse 12 adds: 'For he bore the sin of many and **made intercession** for the transgressors.'

So, intercession means entering the person's world of sin, sickness, or abuse and rescuing them, whatever the cost. It's not easy.

A DIFFICULT CHOICE

A few years ago, I prayed for a man with cancer, and casually said to the Lord: 'I'd like to intercede for him.'

He replied several days later: 'Would you still like to intercede for him?' And I said: 'Definitely.'

But Father's reply shocked me. He said: 'Are you willing to have the cancer instead of him?' It took me four days to answer. But eventually, I said I would.

As it turned out, Father didn't require me to pay that price. But I didn't know that until later. He wanted to test me.

When you intercede, God usually deals with you first, because he won't allow you to pray for something that haven't faced yourself. And it's risky. If you intercede for someone who's in financial trouble, God may say: 'You pay their debts. After all, Jesus paid yours. Sell your car.' Ouch.

Moses didn't know if God would blot him out of the book of life. Paul didn't know if God would curse him. It's a scary step of faith.

CASTING A BURDEN ON THE LORD

Intercession also means bearing one another's burden's. Galatians 6: 2 says this fulfils the 'law of Christ'. Which law is that? Putting others first. In Romans 15: 1, Paul says: 'We who are strong ought to bear with the failings of the weak, and not to please ourselves.'

Soon after I became a Christian, I prayed for a boy who had been ritually abused by satanists. He was deeply traumatised and couldn't talk about it.

One day I was praying, and God said: 'Take his burden, and give it to me.' And I found myself telling God everything that had happened to him. It was awful. I hadn't known the details, but the Holy Spirit did.

That night, the boy slept peacefully for the first time in two years and had no recollection of his abuse. He still doesn't even know it happened.

3. PRAYERS OF THANKSGIVING

Thanksgiving is a lifestyle that unlocks incredible answers. Old Testament priests thanked and praised God every morning and evening (1 Chronicles 23: 30). What a way to start and end the day.

We are all priests now and should do the same – and more. Paul says in 1 Thessalonians 5: 18: 'Give thanks in **all** circumstances.'

I know people from awful backgrounds who are thankful, and others, who have everything, who feel hard done by. It's down to your attitude.

The Bible tells us about a privileged boy named Daniel who had every reason to be a grumbler. He was exiled after the Babylonians invaded Jerusalem when he was around 12. He lost his home, his family, his friends, his royal status and became a prisoner.

But he was still thankful. Daniel 2: 23 says: 'I offer thanks and praise to you, God of my fathers …'

And many decades later, he still had the attitude of gratitude. Daniel 6:10 says: 'Daniel went home, opened the windows, faced Jerusalem, and prayed on his knees three times a day … and **gave thanks** to his God, just as he had done before.'

Thankful prayers will protect us from lions, and unlock God's supernatural world of dreams, visions, and prophecy. They will subdue kings, reveal Jesus in the fire and provide encounters with angels.

THANKS ON STEROIDS

Daniel's prayers were unique. He didn't just say thanks, he **gave** thanks. He is the only man in Old Testament who prayed that way.

The Hebrew word for *gave* is *yedah*, which means *to throw* or *to cast*. It corresponds with the Aramaic word *yadah* which means *throwing a stone, shooting an arrow, or throwing out your hand*.

So, when Daniel *gave* thanks, he threw his hands up to God even though he was well over 70. God likes prayers like that.

Paul was another thankful man. He mentions thanks in his letters to the Colossians, Corinthians, Ephesians, Philippians and to Timothy. He said in Philippians 4:6: 'Do not be anxious about anything, but in everything, by prayer and petition, with **thanksgiving**, present your requests to God.'

He was speaking from experience, because praise freed him and Silas from a grim jail in Philippi.

When I pray, am I thankful for what I have? Or am I always complaining and asking God for more?

OTHER TYPES OF PRAYER

The Bible mentions other types of prayer, too. These are some of them:

- Adoration.
- Confession.
- Lament.
- Deliverance.

It's worth studying them. They will help you expand your relationship with God. He has a different type of conversation for every occasion.

THE POWER OF PERSEVERANCE

Isaac and his wife were childless, just like his father, Abraham had been. But he handled the problem better than his father did. Abraham got a slave girl pregnant, whereas Isaac prayed.

Genesis 25: 21 says: 'Isaac prayed to the LORD on behalf of his wife, because she was childless. The Lord answered his prayer, and his wife Rebekah became pregnant.' We don't know how long God took to answer, but Isaac and Rebekah were childless for 20 years.

The word *prayer* in Genesis 25: 21 means *to dig* and relates to the Hebrew word *pitchfork*. So, even though God had promised Isaac a child by blessing Abraham, Isaac still had to dig in prayer. You may have to do the same.

And the pitchfork shows that God may have to sift your compromises as you do so.

POWER PICKS

- In 2019, the Bunch prayed for a businesswoman, whose company was in financial trouble.

  God showed us that several curses had 'landed' because of some difficulties in the company's past. We also saw a vision of a framed picture.

  The woman said that nine years earlier, God had shown her an image of a framed picture when she had been falsely accused of mismanagement and fraud.

  We broke the curses spoken at that time and work started streaming in.

  God used the picture frame to show her where the curses came from.

- A man in South Africa was bedridden for two years after a fall. But he started to improve when the Bunch prayed. Within a few months, he walked down three flights of stairs and went out with his wife for lunch. And in summer 2022, he went on a 10-day family holiday to Mauritius.

- In 2021, the Bunch prayed for a man with a rare type of cancer. He faced a 14-hour operation to remove his bowel and bladder, several days in intensive care, and at least four weeks in hospital. This is how God responded:

  - A pre-op scan showed the man's bladder was clear and did not need to be removed.

  - The operation was surprisingly completed in half the predicted time.

- The surgeon removed 17 lymph nodes, and only one was cancerous.

- The man recovered so quickly he went home in just seven days.

- The surgeon, who had performed 150 similar operations, said afterwards that the case was 'remarkable' and had never seen anything like it.

- The man has been pronounced free of cancer.

CHAPTER 6

WHY GOD MAY SEEM QUIET

Sometimes, God seems absent and unloving when you need him the most. But I've found that the less he seems in control, the more he's doing.

At times like these, you must stand on the rock of his word, so Father can keep in touch. He will show you that nothing can separate you from his love (Romans 8: 38-39). And in time, he will prove that he works everything for the good of those who love him (Romans 8:28).

Complain to him if you want to. The most honest you are, the better (Psalm 142: 2). But try not to blame him. Blame usually lays with other people, the devil, or both. In contrast, everything God does is perfect. He never fails.

Joshua 23: 14 says: 'You know with all your heart and soul that **not one** of all the good promises the Lord your God gave you has failed. Every promise has been fulfilled; not one has failed.'

This statement still stands today because God does not change. It's as true for you as it was for Joshua. And if it doesn't seem that way, the next verse may sometimes hold a clue:

'If you violate the covenant of the Lord your God, which he commanded you, and go and serve other gods and bow down to them, the Lord's anger will burn against you, and you will quickly perish from the good land he has given you.'

OBEY GOD AS A RULE

Although you are saved by grace, God sets conditions on answering prayer.

To begin with, you need faith. Hebrews 4: 16 says you can boldly approach God's throne. But without it, you remain in the waiting room.

What's faith? It's the opposite of saying: 'I'll believe it when I see it.' Jesus told doubting Thomas in John 20: 29: 'Blessed are those who have **not** seen and yet have believed.'

Faith is quite easy. Hundreds of ordinary people – traders, farmers, fishermen, prostitutes – came to Jesus expecting to be healed, and they were. So, they must have had faith, or they would have gone home sick. They clearly didn't find faith difficult.

In contrast, the educated religious leaders didn't even understand what faith was. There's no record in the New Testament of any of them being healed. Jairus, a synagogue leader, came close when Jesus raised his daughter from the dead.

The word **faith** is easier to grasp if you understand it as **expect**.

You can **expect** Jesus to answer your prayers because the Bible says he will. That's another good reason to read it – Romans 10: 17 says that faith comes by hearing God's word, not his prophecies or his worship songs.

And even if you have faith, God has other conditions. These are some of them:

1. OBEDIENCE

Prayer and obedience are linked. 1 John 3: 21-22 says: 'Dear friends, if our hearts do not condemn us, we have confidence before God and receive from him anything we ask, **because we keep his commands and do what pleases him.**'

So, before you ask for God's help, check that you have done everything he has asked you to do and deal with anything he shows you.

2. WRONG PRIORITIES

God loves answering your prayers. Psalm 66: 19 says: 'God has surely listened and heard my voice in prayer ...' So far so good.

But the previous verse says: 'If I had cherished sin in my heart, the Lord would **not** have listened.' The word *cherish* in Hebrew means to *see*.

So, when you look at your heart, what do you see? A passion for money, position, power, or sex? An obsession with sport, relationships, or possessions? These things can become idols, and Ezekiel 14: 3 says that idols lead to sin.

The consequence? The verse adds: 'Why should I listen to their requests?' This passage was written for leaders, but it applies to everyone. God hates idols.

So, examine your heart, with God's help. What does **he** see? Pray Psalm 139: 23-24: 'Search me, God, and know my heart; test me and know my anxious thoughts. See if there is any offensive way in me ...'

And then? Confess anything that God shows you, accept his forgiveness and ask him to help you change.

3. NOT FORGIVING PEOPLE

Forgiving people is hard, especially when they have badly hurt or abused you. The damage and trauma are very real. But, although you are not responsible for their actions, you are responsible for forgiving them.

Of course, they don't deserve it. But you don't deserve God's forgiveness. To him, we're all as bad as each other (Romans 3: 23).

Forgiving people is costly. But not forgiving them worse. It's like drinking poison every day and hoping the other persons dies. It hurts us, not them.

Matthew 18: 21-25 says unforgiveness locks you out of God's presence and his promises. This leads to torment. I've prayed for people who preferred to suffer cancer, wasting diseases, and mental illness, rather than forgive someone. That's what torment can look like.

Jesus said in Mark 11: 25-26: 'Whenever you stand praying, if you hold anything against anyone, forgive them, so that your Father who is in heaven will also forgive your sins.'

And he added in Matthew 6: 15: 'If you do not forgive others their trespasses, neither will your Father forgive your trespasses.'

This is why some people feel guilty all the time. In God's sight, they **are** guilty. And he can't help them until they forgive. It's a choice. You just do it, despite your thoughts and feelings.

4. MISTREATING YOUR WIFE

God has ways of keeping blokes in order. We need it! So, he says that their prayers will hit a dead-end if they don't treat their wives honourably.

1 Peter 3: 7 says: 'You husbands, in the same way, live with your wives in an understanding way ... and show her honour as a fellow heir of the grace of life, so that your prayers will not be hindered.'

In Greek, *hindered* means *interrupted or impeded by an obstacle like a roadblock.* Many husbands' prayers are stuck behind traffic cones. And only they can move them.

5. NOT PRAYING IN JESUS' NAME

Jesus said in John 14: 14 that if you ask for anything in his name, he will do it.

That seems clear. But many people find it doesn't work and then blame God. But you must understand what it means to ask in his name.

When I was at school, trusted pupils (not me!) were appointed as head teacher's Monitors. They delivered messages on her behalf – in her name. When they arrived in the classroom with a note, it was as if she was there herself.

Similarly, in Roman times, some slaves were empowered to make legal agreements on behalf of their masters. They acted in their name.

So, 'asking in Jesus' name' means praying what he would pray. Jesus' best friend John said in 1 John 5: 14: 'If we ask anything according to his will, he hears us.'

But 'the name of Jesus' isn't a magic formula or a rubber stamp. You must establish from the Bible if it's God's will before you use it. If you are not sure, you can pray: 'Your will be done.'

Let's look at some examples.

Suppose Derek likes Gill and wants to ask her out. Can he pray: 'Lord, I ask that Gill will say yes to a date, in Jesus' name'? No, because Gill has a free will, and God won't force her.

Also, Derek can't tell Gill: 'God's told me to ask you out.' That's spiritual manipulation and sadly very common in church life.

But suppose you want your neighbour to be saved. Can you pray: 'Lord, I ask you to save Terry, in Jesus' name'? Yes, because God agrees. 2 Peter 3: 9 says: 'The Lord isn't willing for any to perish, but for all to come to repentance.'

This doesn't mean Terry will be saved because God gave him free will. But you can confidently pray for his salvation in Jesus' name, knowing that God will answer. He will start speaking to Terry and use circumstances and people to catch his attention.

6. WRONG MOTIVES

God will answer your prayers if you pray with wrong motives – he'll probably say: 'No'! As I said in chapter 2, you won't get answers to selfish requests for 'our pleasures' (James 5: 3).

Jesus never prayed for his 'pleasures.' Neither did Paul. They would not recognise our self-indulgent requests.

Being a Christian means following Jesus' example of selflessly giving to others, not using salvation promises to award ourselves a better standard of living. The issue isn't what you ask for, but what your heart's like. You can ask for £5 with the wrong motive and a new car with the right one.

In the Lord's prayer, Jesus said you should ask for your daily bread. In contrast, some faith teachers encourage you to pray for – or claim – a box of eclairs, and six jam donuts as well.

This is a symptom of a 'me-first' version of Christianity that is based on twisting Jesus' instruction to love your neighbour as yourself (Mark 12: 31).

Many Christians flip the meaning and say: 'You can't love others if you don't love yourself.' But Jesus said that self-love was a problem, not a quality. He said you must die to self (Luke 9: 23) and deny yourself (Matthew 16: 24).

Paul added in 1 Corinthians 10: 24: 'No one should seek their own good, but the good of others.' And his famous passage in 1 Corinthians 13 says that love isn't self-seeking (v5).

Paul also warned in 2 Timothy 3: 2 that in the last days, people would **be lovers of themselves.** This wasn't an attribute. To him, self-love was selfishness.

So, if you ask Jesus for your daily bread, he will give you enough, because you are his child, not because you 'claim' it. But he will probably say 'no' if you ask for more than that.

7. THE ENEMY HINDERS THE ANSWER

Many Christians blame God for unanswered prayers. But he's not the problem. Satan is.

In Matthew 7: 7-8 Jesus described three types of prayers. The first type is straightforward: 'Ask and it will be given to you.'

The second type take longer to answer: 'Seek and you will find.' So, you may have to spend time seeking God before you get the answer.

The third type deal with closed doors: 'Knock and the door will be opened to you.' These can involve spiritual warfare.

When Daniel prayed, God responded (Daniel 10: 12). But the answer was delayed for 21-days when two of Satan's senior officers – the Princes of Greece and Persia – tried to delay it. Eventually, God's Archangel Michael won the day.

The same can happen when you pray. God may send an angel to deliver the answer, but the enemy may try to delay it. And so, you will have to pray to support God's angels, and also fight the enemy. We will look at spiritual warfare in chapter 9.

You don't have to be perfect before God answers you. But he does expect you to do things his way because he loves you. He doesn't change his rules, or dance to your tune. He is Lord.

And so, if he seems quiet, deal with hindrances quickly.

POWER PICKS

- Doctors told a woman to 'expect the worst' before she had a hospital scan and were so concerned, they fast tracked her treatment. But the Bunch prayed, and the endoscopy was completely clear.

- A lady needed an operation to remove a 20mm stone attached to her bladder wall. The Bunch prayed, and the surgeons discovered it had become detached, so the operation was quicker and easier. The lady went home the same afternoon.

- A young woman was healed of long-term fatigue and had the energy to start a children's play group with a friend after the Bunch prayed for her.

CHAPTER 7

UNITED WE'RE HEARD

Many prayer meetings are a waste of time because people are not united. It's more effective to pray on your own (James 5: 16).

Jesus explained how it works in Matthew 18: 19: 'Truly I tell you that if two of you on earth **agree** about anything they ask for, it will be done for them by my Father in heaven.'

He also said that you should sort out relationship problems before you do the spiritual stuff (Matthew 5: 23-24).

The word *agree* in Greek is the root of the English word *symphony*. It means to *harmonise*, so everyone plays the same tune. Then, prayers are answered, and miracles happen. Sadly, many church prayer meetings are a cacophony of bagpipes.

The new church in Jerusalem was like a symphony. Acts 4: 32 says: 'All the believers were one in heart and mind.'

And the passage adds: 'No one claimed that any of their possessions was their own, but they shared everything they had.'

PAYING THE PRICE

So, unity affects your wallet! And there's no point in a starting prayer meeting unless everyone is working towards that kind of togetherness. It comes from changed hearts.

This isn't idealism. There is nothing on earth, in heaven or in hell that can prevent you uniting with other believers if you want to. You start with Colossians 3: 13: 'Bear with each other and forgive one another if any of you has a grievance against someone. Forgive as the Lord forgave you.' Easy enough.

Then, if you have wrong attitudes towards someone, you should confess your sin to God, ask him for forgiveness, and change your behaviour. The other person doesn't need to know about it, and it is kinder and less damaging if they don't.

Then, if you have wronged someone, or they have wronged you, then you should put it right with them **before** you pray (Matthew 5: 24). And you should not tell anyone else. Matthew 18: 15 says you should keep it between the two of you.

If they won't resolve things, then you should involve another trusted believer.

That's all there is to it. Unity isn't something you pray for, it's something you do. After that, Romans 12: 18 says: 'If it is possible, as far as it depends on you, live at peace with everyone.' Then, Jesus will answer your prayers.

However, God does expect you to sort things out quickly. Ephesians 4: 26 says: 'Do not let the sun go down on your anger.' He led by example by dealing with Adam and Eve's sin the same day.

In contrast, in 2003, the Catholic Church began trying to re-solve a rift with the Oriental Orthodox Churches that started 1,500 years ago. The sun set more than 500,000 times on this rift before people started putting things right.

ANIMAL SANCTUARY

I once asked God what true unity looks like, and he said: 'When the wolf can live with the lamb.'

Isaiah 11: 6 says: 'The wolf will live with the lamb, the leop-ard will lie down with the goat, the calf, the lion, and the yearling together.' This verse provides a glimpse of heaven. But it can be accomplished on earth, too.

There are different kinds of 'animals' in your church or prayer group. Some people are wolves, and some are lambs. Others are goats – they always butt in!

Now, a wolf will instinctively tear a lamb to shreds. And a lamb will instinctively run from a threat. And whichever you are, you must deal with any instincts that can cause disharmony. Ask God to help you to change.

In addition, 1 John 1: 7 says: 'If we walk in the light, as he is in the light, we have fellowship one with another.'

Hidden sin affects lions and lambs in different ways. Lions get more aggressive, lambs get timider, and both of their contributions to the praying community are affected.

Now, when Isaiah referred to the wolf laying down **with** the lamb, the word *with* means *equally with* in Hebrew. Wolves and lambs are equal. That's a good place to start building unity.

'OTHER CHRISTIANS? THEY'RE OF THE DEVIL!'

In January 2019, more than 3,000 Christians and a team of respected leaders assembled in London for a day of prayer. But soon afterwards, some groups published statements on their websites, disassociating themselves from things they saw and heard.

They darkly mentioned 'the devil,' 'error' and 'unbiblical practices and beliefs' and then provided public platforms for other Christians to comment.

Many obliged. They hurled abuse and attacked other believers. They either didn't know or didn't care what the Bible says about slander.

Proverbs 10:18 describes slanderers as fools. Amen to that. And churches who put up with them are fools, too. You can't build a united prayer group with slanderers on board.

Proverbs 20: 19 says you should not associate with them. And in 1 Corinthians 5: 7 Paul goes even further: 'Do not even eat with such people.' These are God's rules because he knows the harm that slanderers and gossips cause.

Of course, you should forgive people who wrong you, but you should only meet them again if they demonstrate that they have changed.

The debacle that followed the day of prayer occurred around 12 months before COVID-19 erupted. Perhaps things may have been different if people had preserved unity afterwards. Some people regard the office of prophet as a licence for rudeness.

Agreeing in prayer is a choice, that requires action and constant vigilance.

It helps to start prayer meetings by breaking bread, so that people can discern the Lord's body – other Christians – and put things right if necessary (1 Corinthians 11: 27-30). Then, their prayers will sound like a symphony, and Jesus will answer them.

POWER PICKS

- A baby was fighting for his life in an intensive care unit after being delivered with an emergency C-Section. He was struggling to breathe. But the Bunch prayed, and he survived the night and was discharged four days later.

- A woman had a large mass of bladder stones. The Bunch prayed, and tests showed they had disappeared.

- A woman had long-term mobility problems due to sciatica. But God healed her after the Bunch prayed. She was soon able to walk several miles and even climbed 189 steps in a stately home.

CHAPTER 8

OUR GOD HEALS

Many Christians get disappointed when God does not answer their prayers for healing. But perhaps they didn't read the maker's instructions.

For Christians, healing is usually conditional. God sets out his rules clearly in the Bible, and if you don't stick to them, he may not answer in the way you hoped.

GOD'S FIRST HEALING SERMON

In Exodus 15: 26, God said to the Israelites: 'If you listen carefully to the Lord your God and do what is right in his eyes, if you pay attention to his commands and keep all his decrees, I will not bring on you any of the diseases I brought on the Egyptians, for I am the Lord, who heals you.'

So, Father God revealed himself as the healer in just 52 words. But his instructions included two key points. First, healing is conditional on listening to him, doing what's right, and keeping all his commands.

Second, healing is personal.

Let's look at these in turn.

A CONDITIONAL COVENANT

Healing was conditional in the Old Testament, and still is. Although you are saved by God's grace, his promises to heal you and to protect your health depend on your obedience.

God sent Jesus to offer us a new covenant of salvation that includes forgiveness and healing.

1 Peter 2: 24 sets out God's side: 'Jesus bore our sins in his body on the cross and by his wounds you have been healed.' Matthew 8: 17 confirms that this verse applies to physical healing and deliverance.

So, from God's point of view, Jesus dealt with your sickness on the cross, the same as your sin. You just need to confess and believe (Romans 10: 9) and repent and be baptised (Acts 2: 38) if you choose to.

But then as a disciple, you must keep his commands. That's what disciples do.

However, this fundamental requirement became submerged with the arrival of grace teaching, which said that obedience was legalistic or religious. And it disappeared completely in the post-Toronto over-emphasis on the Holy Spirit.

The truth is, the New Testament contains more than 1,000 instructions for Christians. And God gives us the Holy Spirit to empower us to obey them because we love Jesus (John 14: 15).

There are consequences if you live your own way.

TIME FOR YOUR MEDICAL?

Father invites you to have a spiritual health check every time you take communion. 1 Corinthians 11: 28 says: 'Everyone ought to examine themselves before they eat of the bread and drink from the cup.'

Why? 1 Corinthians 11: 27-31 says that if you break bread in an unworthy manner, you sin against the body and blood of the Lord.

And it adds: 'Those who eat and drink without discerning the body of Christ eat and drink judgment on themselves. That is why many among you are weak and sick, and a number of you have fallen asleep.'

So, for a Christian, communion is either a blessing or a curse. You either affirm God's covenant, or you ignore the conditions and put your health at risk.

Now, not all sickness is caused by sin. We live in a diseased world. Our bodies decay as we get older. Some sicknesses just happen. And God doesn't promise immunity. If he did, you wouldn't need healing!

But if I'm ill, I examine my heart. It's quicker than trying to see a GP and often more effective.

Breaking bread is a key to good health. Christians who don't break bread a lot often sin a lot. And the same often applies to entire churches.

GOD'S HEALING IS PERSONAL

God also said in Exodus 15: 26: 'I AM the Lord who heals you.' He is your personal physician, and he doesn't provide standard healings. His cures are made-to-measure.

The word *heal* in Hebrew means to *stitch together, to cure, darn, mend, repair, to pacify*. These are tasks that must be performed precisely and personally. And God is good at it. Psalm 139: 13 says he *stitched you together* in your mother's womb. He's had plenty of sewing practice.

Verse 14 adds that you are fearfully and wonderfully made. And, with God as your physician, you can be fearfully and wonderfully healed.

If he can count the hairs on your head (Luke 12:7) he can fix every part of your body, soul, and spirit. He knows exactly why you are ill, and how to get you well again.

Father God is a **person** who heals. He isn't a healing force, or a method, where you dig around in your past or tick things off a list. He doesn't expect you to endlessly confess Bible verses. You can teach a parrot to say: 'By his stripes I am healed,' but it'll remain as sick as a parrot, and so will you, if you ignore God's covenant conditions.

He heals you because he loves you.

GOD'S PERSONAL TREATMENT PLANS

I once visited a friend in hospital after he was concussed in a football match. I'm nosey and browsed through the Personal Treatment Plan clipped to the end of his bed.

It said he needed his ankle reset and an MRI scan on his back – an unusual way treat concussion! In fact, they'd mixed up his plan with someone else's

Father God has a Personal Treatment Plan for you, and he won't make the same mistake.

JESUS DID WHAT HIS FATHER DID

Jesus used Personal Treatment Plans. He healed one blind man by spitting on the ground, making mud, and rubbing it in his eyes. Then he told him to wash it off (John 9: 6-7).

But he healed two other blind men by just touching their eyes (Matthew 9: 27-31). And another time, he took a blind man out the village, spat in his eyes and laid hands on him twice (Mark 8: 23).

Each person was unique and needed a Personal Treatment Plan from the physician's son.

Jesus even used Personal Treatment Plans to revive dead people. He waited four days before he called his friend Lazarus out the tomb (John 11: 39). But he merely touched the widow of Nain's son and told him to get up (Luke 7: 11). He did the same with Jairus' daughter (Mark 5: 41).

Later, Peter knelt by a dead girl and prayed, and she came back to life (Acts 9: 40), whereas Paul achieved the same by taking a dead man into his arms (Acts 20: 7-12). Each miracle was different because each person was different.

So, if you're sick, ask Father God for your Personal Treatment Plan and then follow it. It may involve a miracle now, or later. Or it may be a process. It may even include time in hospital. Or it may be a mixture of the three. But you can be confident that it is perfect.

THERE'S NO ROOM FOR DIY

You can't ask God to heal you on your own terms. Namaan, the commander of the king's army tried that in the Old Testament (2 Kings 5: 1-19). He wanted God to heal him from leprosy, and Elijah told him to bathe seven times in the River Jordan. This was like telling him to jump into a sewer.

But Namaan was **VERY IMPORTANT.** He wanted Elijah to come to him and call on the name of the Lord. Very religious and respectable. However, Elijah wouldn't compromise, Namaan capitulated, and God healed him.

In the same way, God may ask you to change your thinking, alter your lifestyle, forgive someone, or deal with wrong attitudes and sin before he heals you.

Jesus also used **Personal Recovery Plans**. He told the demoniac to go back to his family (Mark 5:19), the man at the pool to stop sinning (John 5: 14) and instructed lepers to show themselves to the priest (Luke 17: 14). Again, you need to follow his instructions so that your healing lasts.

THREE TYPES OF HEALING

The New Testament reveals three types of healing. And Father knows which is best for you in each situation. Let's look at them.

1. MIRACLES

All four gospels use two Greek words for *heal*. One is *Ioamai*, which means *instantaneous, miraculous*. The other is *therapeuo*, which means *to cure, heal, or restore to health*.

One or both of these words are used to describe most of Jesus' healings. Miracles were his priority. And we want one, too because they're spectacular and offer quick relief.

But only God knows whether you can cope with the emotional, mental, and social consequences. The blind beggar whom Jesus healed (Luke 18: 35-43) probably had to get a job. The woman who touched his robe had to integrate after years of exclusion and shame (Mark 5: 21-34). The demoniac went back to his family (Mark 5: 19).

God's Personal Treatment Plans only include miracles when he knows you can cope with them.

2. RECOVERIES

The word *Ioamai* (miracle) scarcely appears in the New Testament after the book of Acts. The emphasis is on recoveries.

Jesus said: 'They shall lay hands on the sick and they will recover' (Mark 16: 17-18). And the Greek word for *recover* is *kalos* and means *full well or whole.* It's a process.

It's significant that he didn't say: 'They shall lay hands on the sick and they will receive a miracle.' Perhaps we want miracles more than Jesus does?

3. PART OF SALVATION

Salvation means more than going to heaven when you die. When Peter said in 1 Peter 2: 24: 'By his wounds we are healed,' he used the word *sozo*, or *to save.*

Sozo also means to *heal, deliver, protect, preserve, and make whole.* Physical healing may be part of your salvation package.

So, when you ask God to heal you, allow him to decide how he does it. And don't be discouraged if he doesn't perform a miracle. Instead, thank him that your recovery has begun.

IDENTIFYING BLOCKAGES

Many Christians believe they'll be healed by getting zapped at a meeting, or by reciting some verses. But the Bible doesn't guarantee that. You may get a temporary reprieve, but the healing may not last if the root cause remains.

So, if Father God has not responded to your prayers for healing, consider these possibilities:

1. **YOUR ELDERS HAVE NOT ANOINTED YOU WITH OIL**

James 5: 14 says: 'Is anyone among you sick? Let them call the elders of the church to pray over them and anoint them with oil in the name of the Lord. And the prayer offered in faith will make the sick person well; the Lord will raise them up.'

This firmly places healing in the hands of the local church, rather than conferences or healing meetings.

And if your elders are unable or unwilling to play their part, you should find some who are.

2. **YOU HAVEN'T CONFESSED**

James 5: 16 says that healing can involve confessing your sins to someone else. Few Christians do this, and so remain ill. I've prayed with people who prefer sickness, and even early death, to transparency.

Confessing your dark stuff is hard, but it will get darker if you don't.

It can be difficult to find someone to trust. Churches are not known for keeping confidences. Some people mistakenly share personal information for 'prayer'. In fact, it is often just spiritual gossip.

And leaders often pass details onto their spouses, to be 'transparent'. But they should be transparent about their own lives, not other people's.

You don't need to confess your sin to everyone. Just to someone. And if you can't find someone trustworthy, then seek a spiritual director or a good Christian counsellor. They are legally bound to keep confidences.

Or perhaps swallow your prejudices and confess your sin to a priest! It's your choice – confession, or sickness. But if you choose sickness, don't blame God for not answering your prayers.

3. YOU HAVEN'T FORGIVEN

I make no apology for repeating the subject of forgiveness, because the New Testament does the same!

If you are tormented by physical or mental illness, you may need to ask yourself: 'Is there anyone I haven't forgiven?' There can be a link between unforgiveness and sickness. I speak from experience.

Two years ago, I developed a painful hernia, and God showed me there was someone I had not forgiven. However, I found it difficult, as the physical and emotional wounds went very deep.

But then a friend told me: 'You can either deal with this in five minutes, or five years – it's up to you.' Ouch!

He was right. I could have spent years telling people my sob story, seeking their sympathy, getting counselling, and wasting people's time praying for my hernia. And I would have ended up where I started – in pain, and still needing to forgive the person.

So, I forgave them, and the hernia was immediately healed. When I went to see a consultant, he said: 'This is strange. Your scans show a scar from where a hernia **used to be**.'

Forgiving was traumatic. But the healing was terrific.

4. YOU HAVEN'T DEALT WITH CURSES

The Bible says that curses can cause sickness. Some Bible-believing Christians struggle to accept this. They also struggle to get healed!

In Deuteronomy 28, God warned his people that they would be cursed if they disobeyed him. These curses included:

- Wasting diseases.
- Fever.
- Inflammation.
- Incurable boils, tumours, festering sores, and itching.
- Madness.

- Blindness.
- Confusion.

God also said he would visit the fathers' iniquities on their children and their children's children (Deuteronomy 5: 9). So, curses can affect your descendants. You shouldn't take these verses lightly.

Some people say that a Christian can't be affected by curses, because they were broken by Jesus on the cross. And they're right – Galatians 3: 13 says so. The cross was a complete work.

But no aspect of salvation is automatic. You must work out God's salvation promises with faith (Philippians 2: 12). Otherwise, they remain theories.

Joshua and his armies had to fight for their promised land, even though God had given it to them (Joshua 1: 2). If victory was automatic, they could have occupied Canaan without lifting a sword.

It's the same for you. Jesus has triumphed over the devil and his armies and has given you a land of promises that includes health and healing. But you may have to fight for them by breaking curses and opposing the enemy in the name of Jesus.

Curses don't cause every sickness. But if your condition hasn't responded to prayer, then ask God about it.

I have seen hundreds of people healed when curses are broken. But sadly, many Christians prefer to live with sickness and defeat rather than change their beliefs. And then they say that God is silent.

5. YOU HAVEN'T EVICTED EVIL SPIRITS

Jesus responded differently to people whose health was affected by demons.

He delivered a boy from epilepsy (Luke 9: 37ff) and released a woman from a spirit of infirmity (Luke 13: 10ff). But he did not pray for them. He cast out the evil spirits, and they were healed.

If your sickness is caused by an evil spirit, you won't get better unless it's kicked out in Jesus' name.

Some Christians say they can't 'have' a demon. This is true. They can't be 'possessed' if Jesus is truly their Lord. But the Greek word for *possession* is about *influence,* not ownership. And demons can influence a believer's health.

The woman with the spirit of infirmity was a believer, a synagogue attender and had such faith that Jesus called her a daughter of Abraham. But the enemy had still afflicted her for 18 years.

Not all sickness is demonic. But some is. And if God has not healed you, then ask someone with discernment to pray with you.

WHO IS LORD?

God often heals non-Christians miraculously, to prove he is Lord. He did that with me. But when Christians are sick, **they** may have to prove he is Lord. After all, that's what they asked him to be.

So, if God hasn't responded to your prayers for healing, make sure you have obeyed his instructions. Deuteronomy 30: 11 says: 'What I am commanding you today isn't too difficult for you or beyond your reach.'

His loving commands are truths that will set you free.

POWER PICKS

- A man had been feeling depressed, and the Bunch prayed for him while was in hospital recovering from a stroke. When he was discharged, his wife couldn't believe the change in him. She said: 'I've brought a different man home from the hospital!'

- The Bunch prayed that a business owner would get more clients, as many had been affected by COVID. He got seven the next day, and another three the day after.

- The Bunch was asked to pray for a man who was so ill with COVID that he needed a 'healing miracle'. He got one and was quickly up-and-about and working again.

CHAPTER 9

DON'T YOU KNOW THERE'S A WAR ON?

Many Christians don't see answers to prayer because they don't fight the enemy.

Prayer addresses God. Warfare addresses the enemy. You need to do both.

Paul told us to **wrestle in** prayer in Colossians 4: 12, and to **wrestle with** spiritual forces in Ephesians 6: 12.

Jesus has given his disciples the authority to fight them (Luke 10: 19). Sadly, many Christians never bother to use it. Some don't even believe in the devil, which makes his job easier.

Others try to keep spiritual warfare 'respectable' by saying that praise is warfare. It's not – it's praise. You should use it during warfare, but it's not a substitute.

And many pray **about** the devil rather than fight him. Or they ask God to sort him out, forgetting that he gave them a sword for a reason: to fight!

HOW DOES SPIRITUAL WARFARE WORK?

In Ephesians 3, 4 and 5 Paul laid out some common battle grounds:

- Maintaining church unity.
- Handling relationships between husbands and wives, parents and children, and employers and employees.
- Living holy lives.

And then in Ephesians 6: 12, he said that we don't wrestle with flesh and blood, but with 'rulers, authorities, powers of this dark world, and spiritual forces of evil in the heavenly realms'.

Many people are defeated because they don't fight for what's theirs. So, if your marriage is stormy, you may need to stop wrestling with your spouse and start wrestling with the enemy!

FIGHT SATAN, NOT PEOPLE

Just before Jesus was arrested, he said: 'The prince of this world is coming' (John 14: 30). Now, he could have said that

Judas was coming. Or that Roman soldiers were coming. Or that the scheming religious leaders were coming.

But he identified his real enemy: Satan. That's why he didn't fight the soldiers or defend himself at his trial. Instead, he loved his enemies by calling Judas his friend and healing a servant's severed ear.

Then he forgave them all (Luke 23: 32) and fought Satan on the cross, saying: 'It is finished' when victory had been achieved.

HOW IT WORKS

Two years ago, an orphanage in South Africa faced imminent invasion by gangs that were gathering less than a mile away, blocking roads, starting fires and planning trouble.

The Bunch convened an emergency prayer meeting and took authority over spirits of lawlessness and anarchy, and the gangs quickly dispersed. No one set foot on the home's compound, even though neighbouring properties were affected.

Another time, a woman's life was in danger when she severely haemorrhaged after giving birth. People's prayers weren't answered, so we took authority over the enemy in Jesus' name, and the bleeding stopped instantly.

I could give you countless similar examples. Warfare works. That's why the Bible tells us to fight, and why the enemy tries to stop us.

A BATTLE THAT PRE-DATES TIME

It's easy to sing about Jesus' victory without knowing what it means. To understand its significance, you must go back to the beginning.

Colossians 1: 16-17 says that God created all things ... 'in heaven and on earth, visible and invisible, whether thrones, dominions, rulers, or authorities.' Among them were three archangels, Michael, Gabriel, and Lucifer.

But Lucifer – also known as Satan – became proud and rebelled against God. Isaiah 14: 12-15 and Ezekiel 28: 12-18 recount how God threw him out of heaven. Jesus saw it happen. He said in Luke 10: 18: 'I saw Satan fall like lightning from heaven.'

Hebrews 12: 22 adds that an innumerable company of angels left with him. Revelation 12: 3-9 suggests they comprised one-third of God's angelic hosts.

Satan ended up in the Garden of Eden (Ezekiel 28: 13), where Adam and Eve had been given dominion and authority over the earth by God. But Satan deceived them, and when they sinned, they surrendered that authority to him. He became the prince, or the god of this world (John 12: 31, 2 Corinthians 4: 4).

Jesus eventually came to earth and seized the authority back from Satan by offering himself as a sinless sacrifice for humankind's sin, and then being raised from the dead. By killing an innocent man, Satan signed his own death warrant (Leviticus 24: 17).

And then after his resurrection, Jesus told his disciples (Matthew 28: 18): 'All authority in heaven and on earth has been given to me. Therefore, go and make disciples of all nations.' So, he shared that authority with the church.

But although Jesus defeated the enemy (1 John 3: 8) and disarmed him (Colossians 2: 15), there is more to do. Hebrews 2: 8 says: 'God crowned Jesus with glory and honour and placed everything under his feet … he left nothing outside of his control.'

But the verse adds: 'Yet at present we do not see everything subject to him. But we see Jesus …'

BATTERING RAM, OR BUTTER AND JAM?

So, the church's role is to enforce Jesus' victory in those areas that are not subject to him, by fighting those fallen angels in his name. This is why Matthew 16: 18 refers to the church as a battering ram that breaks down the gates of hell. That's your mission, whatever your ministry.

Sadly, many churches spend more time preparing butter and jam for the next social.

Eventually, Jesus will return to finish the job. 1 Corinthians 15: 24-25 says: 'Then the end will come, when he hands over the kingdom to God the Father after he has destroyed all dominion, authority, and power. For he must reign until he has put all his enemies under his feet.'

But in the meantime, you must fight or face defeat. Unfortunately, Satan does not sign peace treaties.

Yet despite all this, many Christians never fight the enemy. Instead, they fight each other or the world. What a waste of time.

How Satan operates

Ephesians 6: 12 mentions rulers, authorities, powers of this dark world and the spiritual forces of evil in the heavenly realms.

And Colossians 1: 15 also refers to thrones, powers, rulers, and authorities. These are Satan's ranks of angels. But Ephesians 3: 10: says: 'God's manifold wisdom should be made known to the **rulers and authorities in the heavenly realms**, through the church.'

But is the church taking up this responsibility? Or are we too busy dealing with climate change, gender issues and other 'flesh and blood' distractions?

DO YOU REALLY HAVE TO FIGHT?

Many Christians say: 'Yes, but the battle belongs to the Lord' (2 Chronicles 20: 15). But this verse has a different application in the New Testament. That's why I've never been comfortable with the song with the same name. It encouraged the church to sit passively while the enemy took control of the church and then the nation.

Yes, the battle belongs to the Lord in the sense that Jesus has already won it. But you must **enforce** that victory for yourself, your family, and for others. That's why you need armour, and why God has given you weapons.

WE CAN ALL PLAY A PART

Luke 10: 19 says that Jesus gave his disciples authority over the powers of the enemy. So, any Christian disciple has authority over the devil and should use it.

The fight starts with me, and you. We must learn to control our thoughts, emotions, and behaviour. This can be a life-long battle (Romans 7: 15).

Also, problems like divorce, premature death, poverty, and sinful tendencies like addictions come down the family line, the same as genetic characteristics. You need to slay these giants for the sake of your children and grandchildren.

In addition, you may face powers or authorities where you live, or in the sector that you work in.

Some of us fight more than others. 1 Corinthians 12: 12 says: 'There is one body, but it has many parts.' But every Christian has a role in the battle.

THE DEVIL IN THE CHURCH

We are told to test everything (1 Thessalonians 5: 19) and will pay a price if we compromise when Satan appears as an angel of light (2 Corinthians 11: 14).

You must train yourself to discern right from wrong (Hebrews 5:14). This is essential in a confused Christian world that has freely compromised with new age philosophies and the occult.

I know churches who show Harry Potter films to children. Have we gone mad? This brand is repackaged witchcraft, a practice that God calls detestable (Deuteronomy 18: 9-12). Does your church's safeguarding policy cover spiritual abuse? It should.

Some churches teach telepathy and astral projection, and others see 'oil' pouring from people's hands when they pray.

This sounds godly, but the 'oil' is ectoplasm and emerges when mediums and spiritists contact evil spirits. It is not mentioned in the Bible and has no part in the Christian faith.

Similarly, many manifestations attributed to the Holy Spirit are demonic and unbiblical. There's not a single example in the gospels or the book of Acts of Jesus or his disciples responding to the Holy Spirit by twitching, writhing, convulsing, or engaging in uncontrolled shouting, jumping, or falling over.

The opposite is true. In the New Testament, **demons** produced uncontrolled shrieks and shouts (Acts 8: 7) and made people shake, vomit, and fall to the ground (Luke 9: 37-42, Mark 9: 14-29).

It has been one of Satan's greatest accomplishments to convince thousands of Christians that the Holy Spirit causes this godless behaviour.

The Holy Spirit will never make you lose control. Galatians 5: 23 says that self-control is one of his fruits. The Spirit and the word of God never disagree.

SPECTATING ISN'T FIGHTING

Another of Satan's triumphs is turning Christians into spectators. Most meetings, whether Anglican or new church, comprise an audience that watches other people perform.

In contrast, 1 Corinthians 14: 26 says: 'When you come to-gether, **each of you** has a hymn, or a word of instruction, a revelation, a tongue, or an interpretation. Everything must be done so that the church may be built up.'

So, if people don't take part, the church won't be built up. This is why many churches are spiritually impotent. Spectators can't be disciples, since disciples are required to '**Go** …' (Mark 16: 15) And '**go**' means doing something, not watching others do it.

1 Corinthians 14: 27-30 reveals a church meeting where peo-ple clamour to take part. That's God's normal.

OUR WEAPONS

God has given you powerful weapons to enforce Jesus' vic-tory. Let's look at them:

1. PRAYER

Spiritual warfare is only effective when it's used along-side persistent prayer in Jesus' name. You may have to use every type of prayer mentioned in chapter 5 to batter the gates of hell in some situations.

The Banana Bunch sometimes holds 'gate-bashing meetings', where we attack the enemy with prayers of thanks, petitions, tongues, the blood of Jesus, the word of God to achieve breakthroughs. It works.

2. PRAISE

This reminds the enemy who is boss. And God's presence is then assured since he abides in his people's praises (Psalm 22: 3).

But praise must be used alongside other weapons. The enemy may withdraw temporarily when you praise Jesus. But he needs evicting too, otherwise he'll return when the music stops.

3. THE SWORD OF THE SPIRIT

Ephesians 6:12 says the word of God is a weapon. But you need to know how to use it. I knew one guy who waved his Bible at the enemy. But there's more to it than that.

You must find the verses that apply to the situation you are fighting for and then declare them in faith **to the devil**.

So, if you are battling to release someone from a stronghold of poverty, you may pray something like this:

'Satan, I wield the word of God as a sword against you. I declare Philippians 4: 19: 'God will meet all our needs according to the riches of his glory in Christ Jesus' and I use that verse to release Barry from your grip. I declare that 3 John 1 says it's God's will that he prospers.'

And you conclude by using another weapon: 'In the name of Jesus' (Mark 16: 17). It has immense power. When 72 disciples returned from a mission trip in Luke 10: 17, they reported: 'Lord, even the demons submit to us **in your name**.'

The name of Jesus makes demons shudder (James 2: 19) when you use it with faith.

4. GIFTS OF THE SPIRIT

Spiritual warfare is exactly that – spiritual. So, you need spiritual weapons. Paul said in 2 Corinthians 10: 3-4: 'For though we live in the flesh, we do not wage war according to the flesh. The weapons of our warfare are not the weapons of the world. Instead, they have divine power to demolish strongholds.'

That divine power comes through the gifts of the Spirit.

The gift of tongues is essential in prayer and warfare. And you need the spiritual gift of wisdom to fight a crafty and deceitful enemy, plus a gift of faith in difficult situations.

Words of knowledge and the discernment of spirits are essential too, to see and unravel what the enemy is doing.

Christians often tell me: 'The gifts of the Spirit are not for today, brother. They're of the devil.' Then I look at the people who say it. They often live defeated, unhappy lives. They're frequently sick and afflicted with mental illness and have serious family problems.

Some mission organisations and Bible colleges oppose the baptism of the Spirit, and then send young men and woman into some of the darkest spiritual strongholds on earth. No wonder the attrition rate is so high.

DEALING WITH ROADBLOCKS

Paul said in 1 Thessalonians 2: 18: 'For we wanted to come to you – certainly, I, Paul, did, again and again – but Satan blocked our way.'

So, the man who wrote about spiritual warfare didn't win every battle. However, he **could** discern between Satan's hindrances, and God's.

Acts 16: 6 says: 'Paul and his companions travelled throughout the region of Phrygia and Galatia, having been kept **by the Holy Spirit** from preaching the word in the province of Asia.'

Many Christians struggle to discern whether setbacks are caused by God or the devil, or neither. They meekly say: 'God closed the door,' when in fact, the devil closed it, and they missed God's opportunity. At least they have the reassurance that God will work everything for their good (Romans 8: 28).

How do you tell the difference? By testing the hindrance against **God's word**. Otherwise, you end up in an unreliable maze of signs and 'confirmations'. Here are some examples.

You need money to pay for a mission trip. You pray, but the money doesn't come. Is God blocking it, or the devil? 2 Corinthians 4: 3-4 says that the devil does not want people to hear the gospel. In contrast, Jesus said: 'Go and make disciples of all nations.'

So, the enemy is probably hindering the answer to your prayer, and you must bind him, in Jesus' name.

Or, supposing you have booked a course on prayer, but become ill two days before it starts. Is this hindrance from God? Or is the devil trying to stop you from going?

You don't even need to pray. Why would God stop you learning about prayer? Yet I hear Christians in situations like that say: 'Oh, God obviously didn't want me to go.' Strange. Does Father really make us ill in order to guide us?

In contrast, suppose you're applying for a job that means you will have less time for your ministry. The enemy won't block the opportunity, as the less ministry you do, the happier he is. So, if you don't get the job, you can assume that God blocked it, because he needs more labourers, not fewer (Matthew 9: 38).

In addition, James 4: 3 says God will usually hinder self-indulgent prayers to improve your lifestyle, comfort, or social position.

The same applies to church building projects. The New Testament teaches that the church existed to give to the poor, not raise money for itself.

YOUR WILL BE DONE ... PERHAPS

It's easy to figure out God's will, unless you pray with your mind made up. If you do, you are likely to use 'signs' or 'confirmations' to rubber stamp your personal preference.

Many Christians live this way. But John 10: 27 says: 'My sheep hear my voice, and I know them, and they follow me.' It's very simple. Shepherds don't use signposts.

Mark 16: 20 says that signs should follow the word. So, you should allow the word of God to cut through your religious game-playing and demystify God's will by dividing your soul from your spirit (Hebrews 4: 12). After that, God may provide a sign to reassure you.

FIGHT THE GOOD FIGHT

The Bible is a book of God's love. But it's also a book of war against a ruthless, cunning enemy. The battle started before creation, entered humanity in Genesis 3 and continues through to Revelation 21. The question is: will you join in?

POWER PICKS

- A man in America suffered serious heart problems and spent several days in intensive care.

  The Bunch prayed for him, and he miraculously recovered. The medics cancelled procedures to reset his heart rhythm and he was discharged without medication.

- A man in South Africa started walking again after being bedbound for two years following a fall. After the Bunch prayed, he was able to get up and gradually recovered his mobility. By summer 2022, he was well enough to go on a 10-day family holiday to Mauritius!

- A lady with suspected sarcoma cancer in the hip asked us to pray. Her MRI results showed no trace of cancer after the Bunch prayed.

CHAPTER 10

HOW ABOUT YOU?

There's a saying: 'Pray as though your life depends on it.' But this is about **me**. Instead, you must pray as though other people's lives depend on it. Because they do.

BROKEN AND BROKE

Our country is broken. Hundreds of thousands of people are grieving loved ones following COVID. Many are sick. The NHS can't cope. And we are now enduring a cost-of-living crisis. Many churches and Christian organisations will disappear, as I prophesied in 2018.

It's a tragic landscape that will get worse. Most churches ignored God's call for to repent during COVID and so he is sounding his trumpet again.

Our God speaks. He's saying: Pray!

WATCH OUT

Three generations ago, most cities, towns and villages in the UK had watchmen and watchwomen who faithfully prayed. Even three people meeting once a week in a church hall was enough to keep the enemy at bay.

But many churches replaced prayer with projects, music, and socialising. Cynical Sanballats (Nehemiah 4:2) said prayer was 'religious'.

In fact, some in the house church movement said that anything Godly was 'religious.' If you read your Bible, you were religious. If you spent time with God, you were religious. If you talked about the Lord, you were religious. If you refused to have sex before marriage, you were religious.

This absurd attitude from carnal leaders secularised the church and made it impotent.

The result? National devastation.

Deuteronomy 28: 15-68 lists what happens when a nation turns its back on God. We can expect plagues, financial collapse, scorching heat, and drought. Look out your window. It's happening.

It's because of climate change, but it has nothing to do with global warming. Our **spiritual** climate has changed. So, God wants to raise up new watchmen and watchwomen in every

city, town, and village, to pray for people and rebuild spiritual walls.

Cities, towns, and villages are not buildings. They are the
people who live in them. Saved souls save cities. And it starts
with you going into a room, shutting the door, and saying:
'Our Father'.

And then listen. Because Our God Speaks.

Please listen.

POWER PICKS

- A woman had swelling and redness on her arm. The Bunch prayed and she told us the next day: 'The swelling is retreating, and the redness is virtually gone. I put that down to the power of prayer.'

- A woman who was suffering from depression and insomnia started sleeping well and feeling better mentally. She told us: 'I know it's the power of prayer.'

- God healed another woman of back pain the day after the Bunch prayed for her. She said: 'I can't believe the difference in my back this morning, the pain and stiffness feel 90% improved compared to last couple of weeks.'

- The Bunch prayed for a woman diagnosed with Post Traumatic Stress Disorder and she was healed the same day.

ABOUT CLELAND THOM

God healed me of an incurable back condition in 1978 and later said I would be called a prophet.

I have been called many things since then.

But the Holy Spirit has enabled me to bring words and insights to the church over the past 45 years.

I just provide the eyes, ears, and the mouth, and he does the rest.

The results always surprise me.

Despite my fears, flaws and insecurities, Jesus has healed and delivered people, and transformed lives, situations, and churches.

I now help to lead Freedom Church, a praying community that sets captives free. This book is based on our experiences.

Printed in Great Britain
by Amazon

84746869R00072